Living Your Marriage as a Sign of God's Love

Ken Johnson-Mondragón, Editor

California Conference of Catholic Bishops

Nihil Obstat
Rev. Jeff Henry
Censor Librorum

Imprimatur
✠ Most Rev. Jaime Soto
Bishop of Sacramento
July 26, 2025

The *Nihil Obstat* and *Imprimatur* are official declarations that a book is free from doctrinal or moral error. It is not implied that those who have granted the *Nihil Obstat* and *Imprimatur* agree with the contents, opinions, or statements expressed.

Writing team, with the exception of the California bishops' letter, the prayers and blessings as indicated therein, and the pages contributed by *Communio:* Ken Johnson-Mondragón, Molly Sheahan, Kathleen Domingo, and Kim Nickols.

Cover and interior art: Joe Kim
Images of saints and models of married love: see credits on page 66

Published by OSV in 2025. Our Sunday Visitor Publishing Division, 200 Noll Plaza, Huntington, IN 46750; www.osv.com; 1-800-348-2440.

ISBN: 978-1-63966-453-5 (Inventory No. T3067)

Current printing, 2025

PRINTED IN THE UNITED STATES OF AMERICA

RADIATE LOVE

A PRAYER FOR MARRIAGE

Heavenly Father,

We praise you and thank you for your great gift
of the Sacrament of Marriage.

Help all married couples witness to its beauty
through a life of love, joy, patience,
and generous self-giving.

Help families to exercise faithfulness and mercy,
to be one in heart, mind, and body,
accepting children lovingly as gifts from you.

When family life presents challenges
or is lacking in peace and understanding,
teach us the beauty of forgiveness
and bearing one another's burdens.

Strengthen our love so that it endures not only through
the triumphs but also through the heartbreaks of married life.
And bless our homes and our families so that others will see
your generosity and faithfulness guiding our lives.

Deepen our communion at home and with the Church,
so that we may radiate love as a living sign of everlasting hope.

We ask these blessings in the name of Jesus, our Lord.

Amen.

RADIATE Love

"Celebrating Marriage and Family"

Table of Contents

Introduction

Jesus performed his first miracle at a wedding, turning water into fine wine (John 2:1-11), because he believes marriage is beautiful and worth celebrating. The love of husbands and wives images the love of Jesus for the Church (Eph 5:31-32), as both spouses are called to lay down their lives for the other and their children (John 15:13).

The Catholic Church's teaching about marriage is rooted in the example and teaching of Jesus himself in the Gospels, as further illuminated by the inspired writing of Saint Paul in 1 Corinthians 7 and Ephesians 5. As Catholics, we cherish the belief that sacramental marriage is by its nature: indissoluble, faithful, freely given in a mature act of the will, exclusive, and naturally open to new life as a fruit of the one-flesh union of a man and a woman. This teaching is beautiful because it is both good and true, revealing God's design for human flourishing that is patterned on the perfect love within the divine Trinity, adapted to our unique human abilities and longings.

In recent years, marriage has come under extraordinary pressures throughout the world and on every level of society. The best response that the Church, the People of God, can give to these challenges is to support Catholic couples in living their vocation of sacramental marriage, allowing their thriving relationships to stand as an evangelizing witness to God's love in Christ.

While Catholics are already notable for the enduring quality of their marital commitments (see note 5 on page 38), there is always room for improvement. The Catholic bishops of the 12 dioceses of California came together in the 2024-25 pastoral year to provide additional support and encouragement to Catholic couples and families. Under the title "Radiate Love," they invited all families to radiate their love to the world – parents, grandparents, children, spouses, sisters, and brothers.

The bishops directed the staff of the California Catholic Conference to develop a website (www.radiatelove.info) as a curated resource hub for the best tools, programs and materials available to support thriving Catholic marriages. In addition, the staff created monthly resource packets connected to themes drawn from the Sunday readings. The bishops themselves also prepared messages, delivered by video in English and Spanish. These resources help couples, families, parishes and Catholic schools to break open the Church's teaching about the sacramental married life, with practical tips on how to live it deeply and consistently for a lifetime.

The materials in this book are the fruit of these efforts. The reflections, activities, saints, prayers, blessings, and social media messages found here are primarily directed at couples and families. They can be used fruitfully to enrich the sacramental life of a married couple, to provide support and encouragement to parents, to guide a couple preparing to marry, or as a reminder that it is never too late to seek the sacramental grace and assistance of the Holy Spirit to sanctify a relationship that has already stood the test of time.

That said, this book is not a complete guide to the married life for Catholics. There are numerous themes – fertility awareness, IVF, domestic violence, mental health, and addictions to name a few – that could not be adequately addressed in the space of a one-page reflection or a question for discussion. The website has additional resources on these and other topics, as well as tools to assist preachers, catechists, teachers, and youth ministers in their mission to form Catholics of all ages for this high calling (cf. Canon 1063).

The letter from our California bishops is a great place to start. After that, the book can be read sequentially or in any order that makes sense to you. We pray that you will discover "new wineskins" (Mark 2:22) in these pages for the fine wine of true love that Jesus wants to give you, today and always, so that you may **Radiate Love** to the world in and through a lifelong, thriving marriage.

Letter from the California Conference of Catholic Bishops

"The joy of love experienced by families is also the joy of the Church," proclaims Pope Francis (*Amoris Laetitia*, 1).

Thus, in celebration of the love found in marriage and family, we, the Catholic bishops of California, are overjoyed to introduce 'Radiate Love' – a new initiative to encourage and inspire marriage. We are embarking on this journey over the next year to celebrate and support marriage and family life among the flock God has entrusted to us.

The institution of marriage is held dear by God. A marriage between a woman and a man is simultaneously a unique expression of the natural human longing for unfailing love, the source of new life and social health, and a key means by which God provides vital information about himself and human nature. This is because marriage offers a penetrating glimpse into God's identity as a communion of Persons and a model for how he loves us and how we are to love him and every neighbor.

Today, however, many despair of marriage. Marriage rates are declining. It is increasingly seen as an unattainable luxury by poorer and marginalized Americans. And the ties between marriage and children are breaking, with unfortunate consequences.

Observing these losses and offering to help is not a work of nostalgia or an attempt of religion to lecture politics and society. Nor is it an opinion that everyone should marry. Instead, it is a proposal to advance human happiness and freedom, especially among vulnerable groups. It is also a proposal that harmonizes faith and natural reason, and it arises from the same charitable impulses by which Catholic schools educate children, our social services care for the poor, and our healthcare ministries nurse the sick.

Virtually every culture in every age has greatly supported stable relations between men and women and the children they bear. That is marriage. And today, we have overwhelming empirical evidence across the ideological spectrum justifying this preoccupation. Marriage undergirds human happiness, stability, and prosperity. It is the ideal setting to nurture children to a healthy adulthood. Family instability and absent or uninvolved parents – especially absentee fathers – are linked to poverty, crime, inadequate education and employment, and a whole host of other social ills. The decline of marriage is a leading factor in adult loneliness and the growing income and opportunity gaps between racial and socioeconomic groups.

In short, contemporary evidence soundly rejects decades of baseless claims that marriage constrains freedom and happiness, or that decoupling sex, marriage, and childbearing boosts romantic happiness. Most troubling, the uncritical acceptance of these claims often leads to unforeseen disastrous consequences for children.

Scripture strengthens the evidence from natural reason. In the beginning, the Creator pronounces that "it is not good for the man to be alone" (Genesis 2:18). Jesus reaffirms the importance of lifelong marital unity (Matthew 19:6). Saint Paul teaches that marriage offers a privileged entry into the mystery of God's love for his people (Ephesians 5:32). The Gospel reports Jesus' admonition that God's way of loving – faithfully, sacrificially, fruitfully – must also be the measure of human love of neighbor (John 13:34 and 15:8–17).

Saint John Paul II called the family a "school of love." It is where a man and a woman learn to give and receive the complementary gifts with which they are endowed. It is where family members first learn to love those very near "neighbors" strewn on their path – Good Samaritan-style – patiently, enduringly, mercifully, and even in the face of vast differences. It is how we are enabled to share this love with those outside the family and society.

In the words of Pope Francis, the complementarity in marriage and family life is "a great treasure... a thing of beauty." It answers human longing for enduring love, is a boon to vulnerable children, the bedrock of a healthy society, a driver of freedom and social equality, and one of God's most precious gifts to the human race.

With all of this in mind, the Catholic Church in California pledges to redouble its efforts to encourage, celebrate, and accompany dating and married couples through our *Radiate Love* initiative. We invite Catholic couples in all seasons of their lives to engage in their parishes and visit the website frequently in the year ahead. There you will find resources and suggestions to help bring the joy of the Lord's grace into your relationship and family life, just as Jesus brought fine wine at the Wedding of Cana. Please accept this initiative as our gift of hope for marriage and family life.

May almighty God bless you and keep you always,
The Catholic Bishops of California
July 26, 2024 – The Feast of Saints Joachim and Anne

Cardinal Robert W. McElroy Diocese of San Diego	**Archbishop José H. Gomez** Archdiocese of Los Angeles	**Archbishop Salvatore J. Cordileone** Archdiocese of San Francisco
Bishop Joseph V. Brennan Diocese of Fresno	**Bishop Daniel E. Garcia** Diocese of Monterey	**Bishop Michael C. Barber SJ** Diocese of Oakland
Bishop Kevin W. Vann Diocese of Orange	**Bishop Jaime Soto** Diocese of Sacramento	**Bishop Alberto Rojas** Diocese of San Bernardino
Bishop Oscar Cantú Diocese of San Jose	**Bishop Robert F. Vasa** Diocese of Santa Rosa	**Bishop Myron J. Cotta** Diocese of Stockton

RADIATE Love

radiatelove.info

Reflections and Activities for Married Life

Celebrating Marriage and Family

"Many young people today... need someone to show them in a concrete and clear way, especially by the example of their lives, what the gift of sacramental grace is and what strength derives from it. Someone to help them understand the beauty and grandeur of the vocation to love and the service of life that God gives to married couples." – **Pope Leo XIV, May 28, 2025**

In the depths of our hearts, we all want to be seen and known, to love and be loved. Marriage is a radiant gift from God that fulfills this profound desire. While not everyone is called to marriage, this vocation is an integral and meaningful way for us to fulfill the deepest longing of our hearts.

As humans, we use rituals to express meaning that mere words cannot adequately capture. Baby showers, graduations, funerals, and burials are important rites of passage. Likewise, the exchange of vows and rings at a wedding expresses a deep commitment and lifelong promise. Through them, we profess, "I freely give my whole self to you, holding nothing back. I promise to be faithful, and I receive all of you, flaws and all." It's romantic. It's authentic. It proclaims the intimate security that flows from lifelong trust and commitment.

In God's amazing design of marriage, he takes into account our health and well-being. Married people of every background are happier, healthier, and more fulfilled than their unmarried peers, and their children tend to do better socially, emotionally, and academically than the kids of unmarried parents.[1] Marriage is truly a good for spouses, families, and society as a whole!

Make no mistake, marriage can be daunting at times. It can even be challenging just to find a suitable life partner in the first place. Relational, economic, and cultural pressures disorient single and married people alike, and many of us carry wounds from broken relationships, divorce, or traumatic experiences. But when a marriage is able to stand the test of time, it is beautiful, transformative, and ultimately helps us to become the best version of ourselves. This is why we call it a vocation – it is a high calling and a path of holiness that makes us more fully human.

Jesus chose to launch his public ministry while celebrating the marriage of his friends at the Wedding Feast at Cana. This was no accident. Jesus wanted to show us how important the vocation of marriage is to God. Almighty God continues to invite people into the Sacrament of Marriage so that they may radiate his love to a world that stands in great need of such witness.

Prayer Petitions

Lord Jesus, send forth your Spirit to guide and encourage all married couples. May they always cling to one another through the joys and sorrows of life, and may they experience growth and healing to radiate the perfect love of God as the source, example, and final destiny of their mutual love.

God of love, surround the young adults in our network of family and friends with living models of healthy and real married couples and parents to inspire in them a lively hope for a committed, faithful, and lifelong love, rooted in the love of Christ.

Activities for Couples and Families

God's love in Jesus Christ invites married couples to joyfully give witness to the goodness and beauty of married life, inspiring young couples to say, "I want what they have." In honesty, it is not always easy to live up to that call. Join in prayer with your spouse to acknowledge before God the times you have fallen short, then repeat together the words of the leper in the Gospel: "Lord, if you wish, you can make us clean" (Mark 1:40).

Marriage: The Multiplication of Love

"A love that fails to grow is at risk. Growth can only occur if we respond to God's grace through constant acts of love, acts of kindness that become ever more frequent, intense, generous, tender and cheerful." – **Pope Francis, *Amoris Laetitia*, 134**

Throughout his ministry, Jesus attracted a following of laborers, outcasts, sinners, and people seeking spiritual, physical, and emotional healing. With signs great and small, he prepared them for the Good News from the Father: "You are loved! I created you out of love and for love, because I am Love." In his Passion, he fully revealed the depth of his love by offering his life to free us from sin, and opened the door to eternal salvation.

We get a glimpse of this love in sixth chapter of John's Gospel (John 6:1-14). Jesus saw the need of his followers – that they were hungry – and he responded in love. Taking the meager gifts the teenaged boy had brought, he made an offering of thanksgiving and multiplied them to satisfy the hunger of the multitude.

This miraculous feeding was a prefiguration of the offering Jesus would make of his own body under the appearance of bread and wine at the Last Supper. At that moment he announced, "I have earnestly desired to eat this Passover with you!" (Luke 22:15). He was expressing his yearning to give his life, his body, his everything to us – the Church.

For us as Catholics, this is also the key to living the Sacrament of Marriage. Whenever we feel like our gifts are too meager, Jesus simply says, "Show me what you have." Through this beautiful sacrament, as husband and wife we place our lives, our bodies, our everything into the hands of the Lord. God takes our gifts, blesses them like the loaves and fish, and multiplies the love of our marriage – through hospitality, through any children God may give, and through our living witness to God's self-sacrificing love – to radiate love into the world.

Prayer Petitions

We pray for all new or expectant mothers and fathers. Lord, encourage them in their responsibilities as parents, called to witness the multiplication of God's love in their lives.

God of the brokenhearted, bless all parents whose circumstances in life have left them without a spouse. May they experience the closeness of family, community, and your tender love so that they may always know that they do not walk alone.

Activities for Couples and Families

1. The gifts we have been given by God are not meant just for us – they are meant to be shared! Take some time to discuss as a family the blessings you have received that might be meant for the benefit of others. Then sign up to volunteer, serve, or do works of mercy in your community. Even better if you can do so as a couple or as a family!

2. If your children are older adolescents or young adults, it is always a good time to introduce them to advocating for social change and the common good. Contact your diocesan office for life, justice, and peace or your state Catholic conference to learn more about current issues that require advocacy and to find out how you can help.

Who's Keeping Score?

"Christ dwells with them, gives them the strength to take up their crosses and so follow him, to rise again after they have fallen, to forgive one another, to bear one another's burdens, to 'be subject to one another out of reverence for Christ,' [Ephesians 5:21] and to love one another with supernatural, tender, and fruitful love." – **Catechism of the Catholic Church, 1642**

The motto of the Marine Corps is *Semper Fidelis* - always faithful. Marines never leave anyone behind, to the point of laying down their lives for each other. They serve with a willingness to sacrifice all without counting the cost. Similarly, in marriage, each spouse is called to sacrifice by voluntarily putting the needs of the other above their own. That is why Saint Paul invites spouses to "be subordinate to one another" (Ephesians 5:21). Love doesn't hold anything back, present or future.

Even though this can be difficult to live out, when one spouse has difficulties, the other picks up the slack out of love. Couples are called to sacrificial love like Jesus because love doesn't keep score. The couple sacrifices for their marriage because they are better together and joined by mutual respect and trust. In this way, the couple embodies the love of Christ and his Church and becomes an image of God's love on earth.

Marriage is a partnership. Two are united as one, creating a sense of "us-ness" that is greater than either person. Rather than a 50/50 split of child-raising, housework, and finances, it's a 100/100 split of each giving their all for each other and the family. So when money is tight, nights are long, or schedules are stressful, don't keep score. Instead, let Jesus on the cross show you how to love without counting the cost.

Prayer Petitions

God of all goodness, bless each and every married couple, that they might give witness to the truth and beauty of your design for married love, becoming an instrument for the conversion of others.

Loving Father, bless our family, that we may be strengthened in our resolve to form a household of service to you by serving one another and the community, especially those among us who are suffering or in need.

Activities for Couples and Families

1. Noticing and appreciating the good deeds of others in the family builds self-esteem, mutual love, and a sense of belonging. At least once a week, take a moment as a family to name and appreciate a little thing someone did for you during the week.

2. If you have a hard time identifying things to appreciate, it could mean that it's time for a family virtue makeover! Make it a habit (or a challenge) to do something nice each day for a family member without being asked.

Children: The Unexpected Gift

"Children are a gift. Each one is unique and irreplaceable. We love our children because they are our children, not because they are beautiful, or look or think as we do, or embody our dreams. We love them because they are our children." – **Pope Francis, *Amoris Laetitia*, 170**

There are few true surprises left in our instant-gratification world. We have unlimited information at our fingertips, constant communication, high speed internet, and same-day shipping. But there is still one thing that remains a mystery: welcoming a new child into our hearts and into our homes.

Every time a child enters the world, it is cause to celebrate the delivery of an unexpected gift. Sometimes children come before we are ready. Sometimes they arrive when we thought our family was complete. Sometimes a child comes exactly when we had planned, but they appear with unexpected needs, surprising qualities, or special abilities that demand our attention and care. Some children may come to us through adoption, fostering, or as godchildren. Sometimes they leave us too soon. And for some, no children appear at all, even though we may want them very much.

No matter how or when they arrive, children are always a true gift from God. From the first moment of their existence, each is a unique and unrepeatable person with an eternal destiny, chosen and called to become a son or daughter of God through Baptism. Welcoming and loving a child, helping that child to grow in wisdom and faith, is the greatest act of hope in the world. Arriving home for the first time with our new little one in tow, we come face-to-face with a whole new life, a new way of living for another.

Not all are called to become parents. But for the vast majority of us who are, parenting is the primary way we work out our salvation on earth. Each child entrusted to us is also counting on us to help him or her get to Heaven! When we embrace this call, our extraordinary act of hope has the power to transform us through selfless love, tender care, profound joy, and refashioned dreams to become ever more like the Father who created us. No wonder Jesus tells us, "Whoever shall receive a child such as this in my name, receives me" (Mark 9:37). Amen! Thank you, God!

Prayer Petitions

Lord of Life, bless all mothers and fathers who have recently experienced the birth of a child. Grant them all they need to nurture their son or daughter's physical, emotional, and spiritual growth.

Lord Jesus, in your longing to receive every child in Baptism, give us words to encourage our loved ones who have not yet baptized their children. May their little ones be brought to you and receive your merciful love in the sacraments.

Activities for Couples and Families

1. The beauty of God's good creation is all around us, but too often we do not take time to recognize, name, and appreciate it. Organize a nature walk or a picnic in the park with your family, with a goal to find God's fingerprints left behind in the work of creation.

2. Prepare a meal together as a family, making sure that even the youngest members can contribute something. Then give thanks to God for the gift of food and the hands that prepared it.

The Adventure of Commitment

"For those who are not intent on loving forever, it is hard to imagine that they could truly love for even a single day. True love, following the example of Christ, entails a complete gift of self... always seeking the good of the beloved." – **St. John Paul II, April 8, 1987**

Have you seen rock climbers or mountaineers tie a rope to their climbing partner? Ascending to the peak, the climbers entrust their lives to the other person, each one using their strength to pull the other up. Similarly, husbands and wives "tie the knot" of marriage so together they can cross the peaks and valleys of life.

No one knows what his or her spouse will be like in five, twenty, fifty years! Perhaps they will face health problems, job loss, grief, or other great challenges. Perhaps they will still love cooking but have developed a passion for a new sports team, or a talent for dancing. Adventure comes from saying a vibrant yes *to the person,* to a love that holds nothing back for itself and cannot help but say forever. What could be more romantic than that?

Scripture describes God creating man and woman as made for each other in complementarity (Genesis 2:18-24). When a woman and a man freely choose to marry, each reveals a different way of being human through their masculinity and femininity. Husband and wife offer the totality of gifts they have received from God, and God blesses them to become more than either of them alone.

Jesus says in the Gospel, "What God has joined together, no human being must separate" (Mark 10:9). He affirms that marriage is faithful and does not stray, it is exclusive to one's spouse alone, and it is indissoluble, an unbreakable bond. These truths are gifts from God that reflect the commitment to love found in marriage.[2]

The great 20th century author C.S. Lewis wrote, "To love at all is to be vulnerable." Your adventure follows an unknown road, but the journey is worth the risk. God will give you fellow climbers along the way, and way stations when you need support and resources. Together, you help each other reach the peak – climbing to Heaven side by side.

Prayer Petitions

Lord of life, bless the hopes and strengthen the commitment of all young couples who are striving to build a life together by leading them to show by word and deed their mutual love and care every day.

God our strength, stay close to married couples whose journey together is being tested by a rocky road, that they may find confidence to rely on each other in their difficulties and that they may encounter support in the community of faith.

Activities for Couples and Families

1. Every marriage goes through ups and downs. Take time as a couple to name and appreciate how your spouse contributed to a high moment you had together in the last year, and to identify simple but meaningful ways you can prepare together for the next stage of your life together.

2. Make a family visit to – or invite for dinner – a long-married couple you admire among your relatives and friends. Ask them "what is your secret for staying together?" Encourage your children to ask them about the joys they have found in a lifetime together and how they overcame the hard times.

What Does Love Cost?

"Marriage based on exclusive and definitive love becomes the icon of the relationship between God and his people and vice versa. God's way of loving becomes the measure of human love." – **Pope Benedict XVI, *Deus Caritas Est*, 11**

On Veterans' Day, we honor the generous service of our men and women in uniform who have made personal sacrifices to secure and sustain our cherished freedoms here and abroad. Their example provides an important lesson for all of us, that true freedom always comes at a cost that cannot be measured in monetary terms.

Our culture wants us to believe that freedom means being able to do whatever we want, whenever we want, and as much as we want, free from judgments or limitations imposed by any person, institution, or government policy. But being part of a family – whether at home or in our family of faith – reminds us that our choices have an impact on the lives of those around us, for better or worse.

That is not a bad thing. It helps us to absorb Jesus' parable about the widow who gave her last two coins (Mark 12:38-44). Like her, our greatest freedom is found when we give of ourselves abundantly for the benefit of others, even if doing so comes at great personal cost. At its heart, this is a teaching about the nature of God's love. Jesus, the Son of God who literally had everything at his disposal, is the widow who embraced worldly poverty and held nothing back from us out of love. Saint Paul describes this as Jesus' deliberate act of self-emptying and obedience (Philippians 2:3-11).

For most of us, our home life is the setting in which we learn to live and give as Jesus did. There is no amount of wealth that is required to make a loving sacrifice for others. Jesus is our abundance, and his example – brought to life in us through the Holy Spirit – makes it possible for us to freely lay down our lives for others (John 15:13), starting at home. Therein lies our greatest happiness. May we be so blessed as to embrace and live a life of love, no matter the cost!

Prayer Petitions

O Divine Providence, we pray for couples whose dreams of marriage and children appear to be blocked by finances. Bless their efforts and open doors to help them build a life together as a family.

Light of Nations, we pray for all who are called in Baptism to follow Christ, even to the ends of the earth. May the example of his abundant love lead us to respond generously to those in need.

Activities for Couples and Families

1. Jesus reminds us that we must have the simplicity of a child to enter the Kingdom of Heaven (Matthew 18:1-3). Taking that message to heart, the Messy Family Project has issued a *Play and Pray Challenge*.[3] It's easy, and it doesn't have to cost anything. Take the Challenge!

2. At your next family celebration, plan ahead so that everyone – even the smallest children – can share something from their heart with the family and guests. It could be a dish, a poem, a song, a game, a drawing... Be creative! Every person has been blessed by God with gifts, and giving those gifts for the good of others is a beautiful way to show our gratitude to God!

Your Mission, Should You Choose to Accept It...

"Spouses, in virtue of the Sacrament, are invested with a true and proper mission, so that starting with the simple ordinary things of life, they may make visible the love with which Christ loves his Church." – **Pope Francis, April 2, 2014**

At the end of the Gospel of Matthew, Jesus gathered his disciples and gave them the Great Commission: go and make disciples of all nations (Matthew 28:19). Families have a particular role to play: go and make disciples of your spouse and all your children! Admittedly, the mission of the family is not for the fainthearted. It entails sacrifice and sometimes heartache, but all of that is meant to bring spouses closer together and further along the path to holiness. When husbands and wives accept the challenge of married life, their lives build a community of love and radiate that love to the world.

The foundation of the family is love. St. John Paul II even called families "schools of love." In families, husbands and wives marry in love, then see their love deepen through the myriad good times and challenges of a lifetime of marriage, as long as they are willing to accept the challenge. Spouses have the unique mission of helping each other get to Heaven!

Accepting the added challenge of welcoming children deepens our understanding of our own giftedness and dependence on God. Parents are tasked with teaching their children how to be human. What a concept! Through the family, the school of love, children learn most importantly that they are beloved children of God intended to be with him forever in Heaven. Our world today is full of noise and distraction; young people often feel purposeless, unmoored. The mission of the family is needed now more than ever!

This mission, making disciples in our own families, radiates well beyond the walls of our homes. Families, filled with the love of Jesus and love for each other, invite others to experience love and understand their own purpose. Should you choose to accept it, the mission will change you and transform the world!

Prayer Petitions

Most Holy Family – Jesus, Mary, and Joseph – we pray for the parents of toddlers and little children, that you might help them model joy, patience, and enduring hope for these early years.

We pray also for the parents of teenagers that, like Our Lady and Saint Joseph, they may be given grace, patience, and understanding as they guide their children toward adulthood.

Activities for Couples and Families

1. In the Gospel of Luke, the twelve-year-old Jesus asked his parents, "Did you not know that I must be in my Father's house?" (Luke 2:49). Like Jesus, every child of God should learn to feel at home in their parish church. Make a visit to the church as a family outside of Mass and explain to the children everything you see and what it is for. If you do not know what something is called or how it is used, search online[4] or ask the parish staff!

2. Take advantage of breaks from school or special times in the liturgical year – such as Lent, Easter, Advent, and Christmas – to pray, worship, and serve the Lord together. Check your parish bulletin for special prayer and service opportunities, then make plans to participate in them as a family.

Bring On the Wine!

"The Holy Spirit is the one who continues to perform, on a spiritual level, the miracle that Jesus worked on that occasion; namely, to change the water of habit into a new joy of being together." – **Pope Francis, October 23, 2024**

When a young couple falls in love, the fascination they have for each other seems boundless. They want to know every detail about each other's thoughts, experiences, and dreams. As their love grows, everything they ever wanted becomes negotiable to make room for the great treasure they have found in each other. The joy they share is like the "new wine" generously poured out for the guests in the Wedding at Cana.

As time goes by, the pressures of raising children, making ends meet, and the routine of daily life sets in, sometimes leaving the couple to wonder, "what happened to our wine?" In Cana, it took the loving heart of our Mother to notice that their wine had run out. When faced with this dilemma, Jesus' heart was also moved with compassion. He changed the water into the best wine so that the joy of this couple's special day might be celebrated to the full.

The grace that Jesus still offers to couples in the Sacrament of Marriage is the gift of *abundant life* (John 10:10) through a covenant love that lasts a lifetime. It is a daily call to husbands and wives to lay down their lives for each other (John 15:13), discovering the divine joy that flows forth as the "best wine." It should surprise no one that among Christians who regularly attend church, Catholics have by far the lowest divorce rate.[5] The sacramental grace builds on the hard work of making a life together... a constant reminder to return together to the source of our joy in Christ. Who doesn't want more of the "best wine" in their marriage? Gracious Lord, bring it on!

Prayer Petitions

Jesus, Good Shepherd, bless our parish, that as a family of families we might foster a renewed celebration of the gift of marriage and family, encouraging all to celebrate the beauty of this sacrament.

God and Father, we pray for all people whose deep desire to love and to be loved in the vocation of marriage has not been fulfilled. Grant them strength, patience, and trust that their lives are already fruitful in love as they generously collaborate with you each day.

Activities for Couples and Families

1. Fill your spouse's "cup of the best wine." You know what activities or signs of love bring them joy in life. You also know their burdens, the things that sap their energy. Go out of your way to do something special that will bring them joy or ease their burden. Then repeat, as often as you can.

2. Show your children – through actions, words, or both – that love is expressed in many ways, and that there is joy in giving and receiving signs of affection, care, and loving service.

3. Reflect for a moment on the question: How well am I offering the best of myself in the time I spend with my spouse and children? Humbly and honestly share your insights with your spouse without criticizing them in any way, then discuss: How can we be more open to God transforming our ordinary wine into the best wine?

Marriage Is a Trip and God Has the Map!

"God who created man out of love also calls him to love – the fundamental and innate vocation of every human being... Since God created him man and woman, their mutual love becomes an image of the absolute and unfailing love with which God loves man." – ***Catechism of the Catholic Church*, 1604**

Gifted pianists or brilliant pediatric surgeons will often speak of their profession as a calling, a pull in the depth of their hearts that only it can fulfill. It is wonderful to have a career or a passion that is a vocation, but in a deeper way, marriage is a Vocation, a call put on one's heart by God, and a way to love that each person fulfills in a unique way.

In the Sacrament of Marriage, spouses follow the "way" of Jesus (John 14:6), making a generous, irrevocable gift of self. The theologian Hans Urs Von Balthasar wrote, "The inner form of love is a vow." In other words, authentic love is total and forever. Through their vows and the nuptial blessing, couples receive the grace and an outpouring of the Holy Spirit to live out their high calling. Their life in Christ unfolds, and by his grace they become the best version of themselves. And it shows! In fact, married people and their children are more likely to attend church and enjoy better health, finances, life satisfaction, and happiness than their unmarried peers!

Self-gift can seem especially risky in a self-centered culture. Yet God has a plan for each person's life that includes a specific, personalized vocation. God's plan makes the adventure and the risk worth taking. Young men and women should pray, "God, are you calling me to marriage?" The vocation of marriage requires discernment and preparation when young, learning to give of oneself through service, self-sacrifice, works of mercy, and choosing to love especially when it's hard.

If you are married, thank God for the gift of marriage. Give witness to the beauty of marriage by going on a date, talking about your marriage with your kids, and showing the world that this vocation is truly a pilgrimage of faith and hope in love, because God has the map!

Prayer Petitions

Faithful God, we pray for all married couples celebrating a milestone anniversary this year, that they may continue to live their vocation of love as an example to their families and to the world of your faithful, fruitful, and everlasting love.

Gracious and merciful Father, we pray for engaged couples, that they may take time amid the busyness of planning for their wedding day to prepare their hearts for the Sacrament of Marriage.

We pray also for all who are discerning a vocation to marriage: may they recognize the Holy Spirit working in their hearts and respond generously to the call of God.

Activities for Couples and Families

1. Plan a date night out with your spouse – just because! The main thing is to prioritize quality time together in your relationship, showing that you value being together with a spark of spontaneity.

2. If you have older adolescent or young adult children who are not yet married, introduce them to *The Dating Project* movie, the *Humanum Series*, or the *Journey to Marriage* podcast.

3. With younger children, have a family talk to help them to understand that love takes many forms – friendship, fraternal love in the family, romantic love, and God's love that surpasses all others.

Humble Pie

"Neither spouse can expect the other to be perfect. Each must set aside all illusions and accept the other as he or she actually is: an unfinished product, needing to grow, a work in progress."
– Pope Francis, *Amoris Laetitia*, 218

Every marriage relationship goes through stages and seasons, and every couple has to find their own way to navigate the storms that may come. Before the storms start, virtuous habits help form the foundation for love and care in any family. Pope Francis says that alongside please and thank you, an essential phrase for family life is "I'm sorry." Owning our mistakes and trying to do better is hard, but it gets easier with God's help and by forming the habit of forgiveness.

Family life teaches us humility, awareness of our failings, and the things we all need to work on, such as communication, affection, empathy, and prioritizing each other's needs. Knowing when and how to employ these virtues takes time and practice, with a willingness to forgive and encourage when mistakes are made. Jesus reminds us to eat humble pie whenever necessary: "Remove the wooden beam from your eye first; then you will see clearly to remove the splinter in your brother's eye" (Luke 6:42).

Jesus goes on to say that every tree is known by the fruit it produces. In his divine wisdom, God invites couples to deepen their roots, prune the dead branches, and grow through any rocky ground to produce the best fruit. Mutual vulnerability and respect amid differences are the keys to a more profound and enduring love. When the moment arrives to humbly give and receive forgiveness, the Holy Spirit pours out grace on our will so we can grow in holiness and love. Healthy role models and companion couples give witness on how to live humbly and mercifully, and the Church stands ready with a variety of ministries and resources to help you grow together. Don't hesitate to take advantage!

Prayer Petitions

Father of compassion, we pray for all who are impacted by mental health challenges, that they may be blessed with your grace and consolation, and that Catholics everywhere will accompany and support them by promoting mental and spiritual wellness.

Holy Lord, we pray for all families, that through their love and generosity with each other, they may foster vocations to the priesthood, religious life, marriage, and lay ecclesial ministry.

Lord Jesus Christ, we pray for married couples, that you may lead them to understand the gifts of sacrifice and forgiveness as they grow in their love for each other.

Activities for Couples and Families

1. Make a habit of praying with your children at bedtime about how their day went, in a spirit of humble honesty: How were you blessed today? Did you love well? What could you have done better?

2. Talk to your adolescent children about the values and practices that are important to you and your spouse. What kind of person do they want to become as adults? Share how humility and forgiveness have helped you sustain important relationships over the years.

3. Lent is a time of making spiritual sacrifices for spiritual growth, but such sacrifices can be beneficial throughout the year. This year, prioritize the sacrifices you can make for the benefit of your spouse.

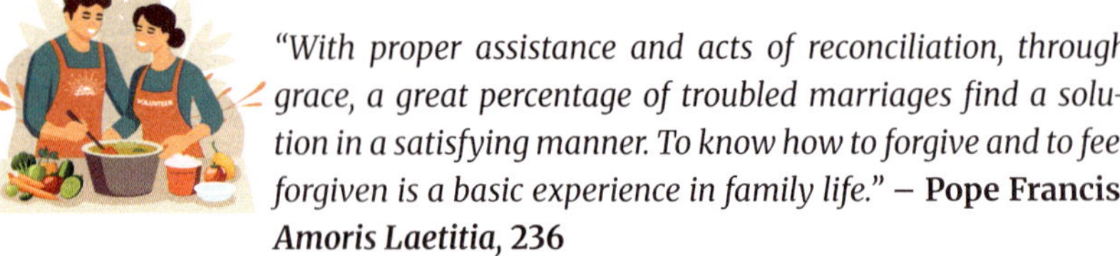

Love Is a Verb!

"With proper assistance and acts of reconciliation, through grace, a great percentage of troubled marriages find a solution in a satisfying manner. To know how to forgive and to feel forgiven is a basic experience in family life." – **Pope Francis, *Amoris Laetitia*, 236**

Have you ever watched closely the faces of a bride and groom on their wedding day? They are full of wonder and hope, envisioning a lifetime of joy and love ahead. Exactly as they should be! What about the faces of a husband and wife who celebrate their 50th wedding anniversary? The look they share is a knowing one, rich with shared memories, past hurts, unexpected joys, and the great gift of being known and loved deeply. To get from the first glance to the latter requires a commitment that is not a fleeting fancy or a shifting emotion. Jesus taught us to reconcile with those we have offended (Matthew 5:24) and always forgive those who have offended us (Luke 6:37). Asking for forgiveness regularly actually deepens one's love.

Love – true love – is a verb! Love is a decision made every single day, sometimes every minute, to actively place the needs of your beloved ahead of your own. This is not easy, but as Christians we find our inspiration for marital love in Scripture. The love between husband and wife points to the love between Jesus and his Church, the People of God. Jesus lays down his life for each of us, and his last words on the cross were to ask forgiveness for those who put him to death.

Most of us will never be asked to actually lay our lives down for our spouses. But in our difficult moments, it sometimes feels like it! Small slights and unspoken pain can yield resentment, and we may find ourselves wondering what we ever found so lovable about our spouses in the first place! Psalm 126 holds the key. The Israelites cry out, "The LORD has done great things for us!" even though they had just spent decades in exile, away from their promised land. If you ever feel abandoned, lonely, or unseen in marriage, return to this scripture passage to reassure yourself of God's constant love. Then address your difficulties together with a spirit of patience and kindness, asking for each other's forgiveness. If necessary, seek the help of a Catholic counselor. The result will have you both seeing the great new things the Lord can do for you as he opens a way through the wilderness (Isaiah 43:19).

Prayer Petitions

Christ the Healer, we pray for families who suffer due to illness, poverty, violence, mental health challenges or other hardships, that they may find peace and renewed strength in you.

God of steadfastness and encouragement, we pray for all couples struggling in their marriages, that they may entrust themselves and their family to your loving hands.

Father of the fatherless, we pray for all those suffering from troubled or broken marriages, including children, that they may be assured of your unfailing tenderness toward them.

Activities for Couples and Families

1. In marriage, unsatisfying habits in the relationship can cause frustration or resentment to build over time. Take it to prayer together! Ask the Lord to do something new in your hearts this month to help you love each other better here and now.

2. Too often, children see their parents argue, but they never see the resolution or forgiveness that takes place in private. Talk to them about how God helps spousal love to grow through disagreements when each person admits their faults and asks for forgiveness.

3. Jesus was a master at setting boundaries and inviting his followers to make the best choices. Tune up your approach to forming your children with the free *Discipline Guide*[6] from the Messy Family Project.

Honoring All Mothers

"The loveliest masterpiece of the heart of God is the heart of a mother." – **St. Thérèse of Lisieux**

The sheep know the voice of the Good Shepherd, who seeks the lost ones, even in the middle of the night. Good moms are similarly attuned, listening for the needs of their child(ren) and sacrificing sleep and comfort for their sake. Motherhood mirrors the unconditional love of God, making personal sacrifices as a sincere gift of self. And, like the Good Shepherd, moms rejoice each time they reconnect with their children and deepen their bonds of love.

Motherhood can often be an under-celebrated vocation. Much mothering is done discreetly – comforting little one's hurts, serving as tutor, chef, coach, advisor, and launching young adult children into their own lives, separate but ever-connected. In each of these moments of motherhood, women tap into the gifts of their femininity that provide strength and compassion, nurturing and encouragement. Moms find fulfillment in the small moments – a homemade gift, a tight hug, and a quick kiss from kids big and small.

Still, our culture can and must do more to support motherhood, which in many ways is losing social standing. In a world where people are seen as interchangeable, the incomparable bond between mother and child is sometimes sidelined. Yet, as we learn the Gospel, the voice of the Shepherd is unique and unrepeatable (John 10:27). So too the voice of a mother to her children. Newborns already know the voice of their mothers whose bodies have housed them for nine months, and it is mothers who first present children to the world, including to the new father, and teach them about belonging, community, love, and responsibility.

Today we pray for all moms to receive the grace they need to be the best examples of life-giving, sacrificial love to their children.

We show our gratitude for the countless moments of comfort and support that moms give. And we give thanks for all mothers as a visible image of God's love in the world.

Prayer Petitions

Lord Jesus Christ, we pray for mothers whose unconditional love for their children, in moments of joy and difficulty, mirrors your love for the Church. Grant that they may be given the grace to be true witnesses to the Gospel message, enthusiastically accepting the challenge of forming the next generation of saints.

We pray for all mothers – including godmothers, grandmothers, stepmothers, birth mothers, adoptive mothers, foster mothers, spiritual mothers, and those who mother in any way – that they may be supported and encouraged in their special vocation of love.

God of consolation and peace, we pray for mothers mourning the loss of a child, that they may grieve and find healing, comforted by the hope that they will one day be reunited with their child in Heaven.

Activities for Couples and Families

1. As a way to show care for the mother in your family, put your heads together to identify what is most stressful in her life right now and devise a way to relieve that stress in a meaningful and ongoing way.

2. Make a plan for a fun family activity with quality time together. In the midst of it, take time to express from your heart the many things you love and appreciate about her presence in your life.

The Love of the Father

"If love reigns in our heart, we become, in a complete and luminous way, the persons we are meant to be... In the deepest fiber of our being, we were made to love and to be loved." – **Pope Francis, *Dilexit Nos*, 21**

There is a close connection between our celebrations of Trinity Sunday and Father's Day, which occur around the same time each year. As human beings, we are created in the image and likeness of God, who is an eternal, loving communion of divine persons – the Holy Trinity. In the words of Saint Augustine, the Father loves the Son, the Son receives the love of the Father and responds with love in return, and the Holy Spirit *IS* the love that unites them! In a similar though unique way, spouses give and receive the love of the other, and their love has the incredible power to create a child! It is this generous, self-giving love that makes a man a true father.

Jesus himself revealed to us that God is our Father, our "Abba." And Saint Paul reminds us that our Christian understanding of family comes from the fatherhood of God the Father (Ephesians 3:14-15). Social science has definitively shown that the optimal setting for children to grow and develop is within a stable and loving family headed by their biological mother and father.[7] In a world where nothing is perfect, we rightly do our best to nurture children in every circumstance, yet these facts remind us that fatherhood is integral to God's plan for humanity. He sees our longing for the tender love, mercy, protection, and example of a good father. Jesus also reveals the generosity fathers are called to in the Gospel when he confidently says, "Everything that the Father has is mine" (John 16:15). It is the exact opposite of the uncertainty of the prodigal son (Luke 15:11-32).

Fathers who embrace their massive task of generous self-gift imitate God's love by giving of themselves continuously, generously, sacrificially, and completely for the material and spiritual well-being of their spouse and children. In so doing, they help us to comprehend the love of our Heavenly Father, who lovingly and heroically gave everything for us through his only begotten Son, welcoming us into his own divine life in the Holy Spirit. So as we worship the Father, the Son, and the Holy Spirit, we pray that the Triune God of love will also bless our fathers and fathers-to-be, forever and ever. Amen!

Prayer Petitions

Heavenly Father, encourage and support all fathers in their role as primary educators and models of Christian living for their children.

We pray also for married couples, that they may reflect the love of the Trinity in their homes, to their families, and to their friends.

Living God, unite our parish as a family of families, that we may find ways to care for our married couples and support the fathers, mothers, and families among us who are the domestic church.

Activities for Couples and Families

1. Most families have customs to show appreciation and care for the fathers in their lives – special gifts, hand-made crafts, a day of relaxation, a nice meal of their favorite foods, etc. Try adding a spiritual dimension to your celebration. Pray the *Prayer for Fathers* (p. 84) over him and show your appreciation for him by asking him to share some special memories from his childhood or youth.

2. Watch a movie together that celebrates fatherhood, then talk about the sacrifices fathers make for their children and the purpose or meaning it gives to their lives. Some possibilities include: Finding Nemo, Mrs. Doubtfire, The Way, Father of the Bride, The Pursuit of Happyness, Life is Beautiful, We Bought a Zoo, Field of Dreams, Minari, or Fatherhood. You may want to check out the reviews on PluggedIn.com or CommonSenseMedia.org to make sure that your selection is age-appropriate for your kids.

Notes

[1] U.S. Department of Health and Human Services, Office of Planning, Research & Evaluation, "Success Sequence: A Synthesis of the Literature" (https://www.acf.hhs.gov/opre/report/success-sequence-synthesis-literature).

[2] For those who know the pain of divorce, that deep suffering speaks the truth that no one was meant to go through such a loss. If that is your story, know that there is healing for you. The Church offers great solace and spiritual growth for those who separate or divorce.

[3] https://messyfamilyproject.org/challenge/.

[4] For example, https://www.youtube.com/watch?v=HtXqm5N1vaA and https://www.youtube.com/watch?v=rtP3C3HJImY.

[5] An analysis of General Social Survey (GSS) data in the United States since 1998 shows that among people age 40 or older who had ever been married, only 31% of Catholics had ever been divorced while 44% of all other Christians and 47% of people without any religious affiliation had ever divorced. The statistical margin of error was about ±1% in each case.

Among ever-married Catholics over age 40 who regularly attended Mass, the ever-divorced rate was only 20%, compared to 35% for other Christians who regularly attended worship services, with a margin of error of about ±2%. This puts the divorce rate of Catholics at 30% to 45% lower on average than that of other Christians.

[6] https://messyfamilyproject.org/guide/discipline-guide/.

[7] Many research studies continue to bear this out, frequently highlighted in reports by the Institute for Family Studies (ifstudies.org). A prominent journal article summarized the research in 2010: Susan L. Brown, Journal of Marriage and Family, "Marriage and Child Well-Being: Research and Policy Perspectives," October, 2010 (https://pmc.ncbi.nlm.nih.gov/articles/PMC3091824/).

Saints and Models of Married Love

Saint Thomas More: Martyr for the Sacrament of Marriage

Born in London in 1478 as the son of a prominent lawyer and judge, Saint Thomas More received a classical education and pursued higher studies in law. He would become a prominent public servant in his own right, renowned for his brilliance and moral honesty. He married Jane Colt of Essex in 1505, and they had four children together. When she died of a sudden illness in 1511, he quickly married a widow named Alice Middleton so that his children would not long suffer the lack of a loving mother. Their home was always open to others in need, especially children – they welcomed two girls as wards and raised them as their own.

When King Henry VIII declared himself "Supreme Head of the Church," Saint Thomas opposed the king's designs, especially with regard to divorce. He refused to take an oath acknowledging the children of King Henry and Anne Boleyn as legitimate heirs to the throne, so he was accused of treason and sentenced to death by beheading in 1534. Thus, he became a martyr for the Sacrament of Marriage.

Questions for Couples

How does the example of Saint Thomas More and his wives Jane and Alice inspire or challenge us to grow in our marital commitment and love? How are we called to nurture the life of the next generation?

Questions for Parents and Children

Think of the married couples you know. Which ones are good role models for marriage? How can your family learn from them to grow in sensitivity and service to those in need?

Blesseds Luigi and Maria Beltrame Quattrocchi: Family Life as a Path of Holiness

Blesseds Luigi and Maria Beltrame Quattrocchi lived in Rome in the first half of the 20th century, keeping the light of faith burning in their family life through prayer and devotion to the Eucharist. When asked about their four children, Maria responded quickly and honestly, "We brought them up in the faith, so that they might know and love God."

Drawing on Scripture and the lives of the saints, Luigi and Maria found ways to develop a rich spirituality, both as spouses and as parents. They generously dedicated themselves to teaching and guiding their children to discover God's plan of love for their lives. Saint John Paul II noted that their exemplary home life brought forth vocations to the priesthood and the consecrated life, showing that marriage and the religious life are complementary since they both have roots in the same spousal love of Christ.

Questions for Couples

How and in what circumstances do we experience closeness to God in our married life? What more can we do to cooperate with God's plan of love for us as a couple?

Questions for Parents and Children

As you look around the world today, what do you see that is good about being married? Share with your children how your faith helps you to overcome challenges and find joy in your marriage.

Saint Lorenzo Ruiz: Patron of Migrants, the Philippines, and Separated Families

Saint Lorenzo Ruiz was born in 1596 to a Filipino mother and Chinese father. Raised in Manila, Lorenzo served his parish, had a strong devotion to the rosary, and wound up marrying a woman named Rosario! The happy couple lived a peaceful, prayerful life with their two sons and one daughter. The daily lessons and prayer life they practiced as a family strengthened them for the crosses ahead.

In 1636, Lorenzo was falsely accused of killing a Spaniard and was forced to flee to Japan. Shortly after arriving in Nagasaki, Lorenzo and the priests he was with were arrested by the shogunate, brutally tortured for their faith, and martyred. Although he was tempted to renounce his faith, Lorenzo's last words were "Had I one thousand lives, all of these I would give to God."

Lorenzo and Rosario faced many terrible challenges that couples experience even to this day: racism, separation, loss of a spouse, forced migration, persecution for the faith. They can be great intercessors for couples and families to persevere in hard times.

Questions for Couples

What crosses do we carry as a couple, or as a family? How does our faith help us carry those crosses? How can we strengthen our prayer life to imitate the Ruiz's?

Questions for Parents and Children

Most people in our country will never have to face death for our beliefs, but we all have to make sacrifices sometimes for our family. Which sacrifices are especially hard for you? How does it feel when you generously do something nice for someone in your family?

Venerable Pierre Toussaint: A Heart for Children in Need

Venerable Pierre Toussaint (1766-1853) was born a slave in Haiti and died as a freeman in New York City. In his early 20s, Pierre was brought to New York City enslaved by the Berard family, who apprenticed him to a local hairdresser. Pierre learned the trade quickly and eventually worked very successfully in the homes of rich women in New York City. Toussaint attended daily Mass for 66 years at St. Peter's in New York.

When Mr. Berard died, Pierre became the breadwinner for himself, Mrs. Berard, and the others enslaved in the household. He was freed shortly before Mrs. Berard's death in 1807. Four years later, he married Marie Rose Juliette, whose freedom he had purchased. They later adopted Euphémie, his orphaned niece. Together, the Toussaints began a career of charity and philanthropy among people experiencing poverty, such as starting the city's first school for Black children. They raised money for Old St. Patrick's Cathedral, and sheltered orphans and fostered numerous boys in succession, supporting them in learning a trade. He is considered to be the father of Catholic Charities in New York.

Questions for Couples

How do we share the blessings we have received with others in need, especially children? What more can we do to form the hearts of our own children for service?

Questions for Parents and Children

How do you think it felt for Venerable Pierre to grow up as a slave? And then to be freed? Venerable Pierre and Marie Rose did not have any children of their own. Why do you think they cared and sacrificed so much for other people's children?

Our Lady, Untier of Knots

Saint Irenaeus wrote in the 2nd century, "The knot of Eve's disobedience was untied by the obedience of Mary. What the virgin Eve bound by her unbelief, the Virgin Mary loosened by her faith." (*Adversus Haereses,* III, 22, 4) Mary's yes to being the mother of Jesus and her life lived according to God's will untied for all the knots of sin and death. From the earliest days of the Church, Mary has helped her children untangle the knots in their lives, whether knots of sin, discord, hurt, doubt, or anything that troubles them. Jesus is the Savior, and Mary intercedes for us to her Son.

In 1700, a Bavarian artist was commissioned by Fr. Hieronymus Langenmantel to paint Our Lady Untier of Knots in thanksgiving for the restoration of his grandparents' marriage through her intercession. To this day, her shrine receives hundreds of thousands of pilgrims. Devotion spread from there to Brazil and Argentina. Today, Pope Francis' strong devotion to Our Lady Untier of Knots has introduced millions to our mother under this special title. Our Lady, Untier of Knots, pray for all married couples, especially those facing difficulties.

Questions for Couples

What are the knots in your married life or family life that need to be untied? How can you support each other in prayer and loving service to overcome those knots?

Questions for Parents and Children

Parents, tell your children about a time when you needed your mother's help to get out of a tricky situation. How did you feel? What knots do you see in the world around you? How can your family help untie each other's knots with Mary's intercession?

Venerable Vittorio Trancanelli: The Saint of the Operating Room

Born in 1946 in Perugia, Italy, Vittorio Trancanelli was a devoted surgeon known as "the saint of the operating room." He offered medical care regardless of patients' ability to pay and showed deep empathy, particularly for children and those with disabilities. Married to Rosalia in 1964, they had two biological and seven adopted children, many with severe disabilities.

They also welcomed women and children in need into their home as a refuge. Despite suffering from peritonitis, Vittorio continued to serve others selflessly. He embodied sacrificial love, both in his medical career and family life, often reflecting "It is true that welcoming is not always easy, sometimes it is tiring, but the Lord tells us: 'If I, the Lord and the Master, have washed your feet, then you too must wash each other's feet.'" (John 13:14)

Questions for Couples

Who are the people in your life who exhibited empathy? What did you learn from them that has helped you? Think of a time when both of you made a sacrifice out of love, or served the other. How did that help your relationship grow?

Questions for Parents and Children

Vittorio was sick for many years, yet he used his own pain to have empathy for others in need including his family. How do you think he was able to do that? Can you think of a time when someone in your family made a sacrifice to help out? How did that make you feel?

The Holy Family: Model for All Christian Families

The Holy Family – Jesus, Mary, and Joseph – are the perfect model for all Christian families. In their home, love was taught through example. Joseph's protective care and Mary's nurturing presence created a secure environment to lead their child to the house of the Heavenly Father. Mary and Joseph raised Jesus as devout Jews, praying together as a family, reading the Hebrew Scriptures, teaching him the carpentry trade.

They suffered together too, from Jesus' birth in a stable, to fleeing persecution as migrants in Egypt, to losing Jesus for three days in the Temple. In all joys and sorrows, the Holy Family lived the virtues of diligence, humility, and compassion. Living in obscurity in Nazareth, they raised Jesus "to grow in wisdom, and age, and favor with God and man" (Luke 2:52). It was in the love of their home that Jesus' mission on earth would blossom.

Questions for Couples

How can you ensure that your relationship and family life reflect the love exemplified by the Holy Family? What kind of legacy do you want to create together, not only within your own family but also in your community?

Questions for Parents and Children

How is your family similar to the Holy Family in how you learn, pray, and serve? How is your family different? How can your family continue to grow in virtue like the Holy Family?

Patriarchs Tobiah and Sarah: Faith in God's Providence

In the Book of Tobit, Tobiah journeys to Media along with the Archangel Raphael, the patron of marriage and healing. There, Tobiah meets Sarah and falls in love with her. But Sarah is plagued by a demon named Asmodeus, who has killed seven of her previous husbands on their wedding nights. Even as she suffered each loss, she was falsely accused of killing her husbands, which only served to compound her grief.

Her parents give Tobiah permission to marry Sarah, encourage them, and pray for them. The newlyweds kneel in prayer in their bedroom, offering a burnt sacrifice to drive away the demon. Tobiah asks for God's blessing, that they may help each other like Adam and Eve with sincere love. "Grant that I may find mercy and may grow old together with her" (Tobit 8:7). When they awake in the morning, the demon is gone, and the whole family praises God for his mercy and compassion. Tobiah and Sarah are a beautiful example of healing in marriage, and faith in God's providence.

Questions for Couples

In what ways do you see patterns of discord or the trappings of the evil one in your marital relationship? Take it to prayer together. Where do you see God pouring out the new wine of his grace in your personal relationship and family life?

Questions for Parents and Children

Through prayer and humbly following God's will in their lives, Tobiah and Sarah experienced an abundance of God's blessings. How has he blessed your family? What good gifts has he given you? How might you share those gifts with others who are in need?

Saints Louis and Zélie Martin: Perseverance in Hardship

Saints Louis and Zélie Martin, parents of Saint Thérèse of Lisieux, are celebrated for their exemplary Christian marriage and family life. Born in Bordeaux, France, in 1823, Louis became a watchmaker, while Zélie, born in 1831 in Gandelain, mastered lace-making and ran a successful business. Both initially felt called to religious life but found in each other a different vocation.

They met in 1858, married three months later, and quickly formed a strong spiritual bond. The Martins had nine children, though four died in infancy. Zélie found comfort in the Lord, saying, "We shall find our little ones again up above." She balanced motherhood with her business until she passed away from breast cancer at age 46. Louis carried on raising their five daughters in the faith, all of whom later entered religious life. They in turn cared for him when he struggled with dementia in his later years. Louis and Zélie were canonized in 2015.

Questions for Couples

Saints Louis and Zélie balanced work, family life and faith. They had great joys but also great hardships in their marriage. What can the lives of Louis and Zélie teach you about becoming saints as a married couple?

Questions for Parents and Children

As a single father with five daughters ages 4 to 17, Saint Louis made sure they all worked together to meet everyone's needs. His daughters then made sure his needs were met in old age. What does that say to you about the importance of caring for one another as a family? What more are you each called to do for one another?

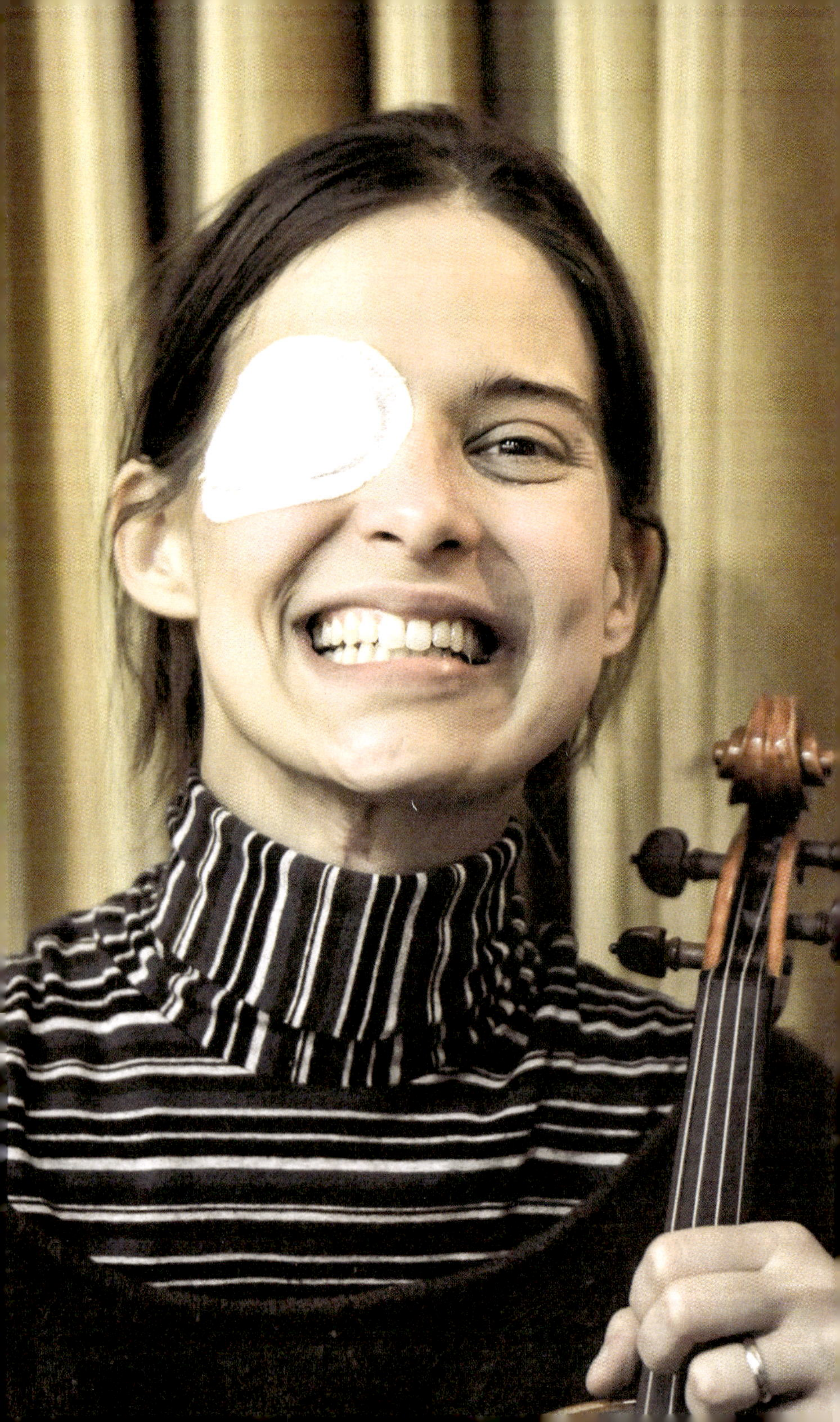

Servant of God Chiara Corbella Petrillo: A Life-Giving Love

Chiara Corbella, born January 9, 1984, in Rome, Italy, met her husband Enrico on a pilgrimage, and both were active in the charismatic renewal. When their first two children, Maria and Davide, were diagnosed with life-limiting conditions in utero, Chiara and Enrico chose to carry and cherish them for the duration of their short lives. Both children passed away shortly after their birth. Chiara shared her experience of welcoming her children at church events, speaking about the gift their lives represented.

During her third pregnancy, Chiara was diagnosed with a cancer of the tongue. She chose treatments that would protect both her and her unborn son, Francesco, who was born healthy. Despite her illness, Chiara radiated joy and faith. In fact, this photo of her was taken in April 2012, just days after her terminal diagnosis. She passed away on June 13, 2012. Chiara is an outstanding example of hope and trust in the promise of the resurrection.

Question for Couples

Heroic love like Servant of God Chiara is never just a spontaneous choice – it is the fruit of a lifetime of practice. What are some specific ways you can show your love for each other better this week?

Question for Parents and Children

Human life is God's most precious gift to us! What are some of the things you most appreciate about the gift of having each other as a family? Make it a habit to tell each other these things!

Saint Agnes Lê Thị Thành: Trust in God, Come What May

Saint Agnes Lê Thị Thành was born into a devout Catholic family in 1781 in the north of Vietnam. Her feast day is July 12, commemorating the day of her death in 1841. She married and raised two sons and four daughters in the faith in the midst of a great religious persecution, and she sheltered priests in her home to offer the sacraments in secret.

Eventually, St. Agnes was caught and arrested at age 60 during a raid for Catholic priests. She was beaten, tortured, and even had venomous snakes put in her clothes. Yet she courageously witnessed to her children, urging them to keep the faith, and told her husband, "I entrust the children to you, trust in God. As for me, I will trust and follow Jesus to the end." She died as the only non-clergy woman among the 117 Vietnamese martyrs for the faith.

Questions for Couples

What kinds of habits of faith does our family practice (prayer, service, attending Mass, reading scripture, forgiveness, talking about God, etc.)? How can we strengthen our faith together to be more like St. Agnes in our daily lives?

Questions for Parents and Children

St. Agnes showed by the example of her life that love is more than a feeling – it is a verb that needs to be demonstrated in action and sometimes requires sacrifice. What does it mean for us as a family that love is a verb? What more can we do to put our love for each member of our family into action?

Saint Monica: The Power of Prayer in the Face of Adveristy

Saint Monica was a devout Christian born in 4th-century Algeria. Married to Patricius, a non-believer, she navigated his emotional abuse and unfaithfulness as best she could. She prayed fervently for his conversion which finally came just a year before his death.

Her greatest struggle was her son, Augustine, who rejected Christianity, joined Manichaeism, lived with a mistress, and fathered a child outside marriage. For nearly 20 years, Monica prayed persistently for his conversion, once hearing from a bishop, "The child of those tears shall never perish."

She practiced tough love but ultimately chose to stay close to Augustine, urging him toward good influences, like St. Ambrose. Her prayers were answered in 387 when Augustine converted to Christianity. Monica died later that year, witnessing her son's transformation into a theologian and Doctor of the Church. She remains a model of patience and the power of prayer in adversity.

Questions for Couples

Motherhood is sometimes viewed in our culture as a cross, or worse, a limit on our personal ambitions. How do the examples of the Blessed Virgin Mary, St. Monica, and other mothers we know show us the power of motherhood to enter into the love of God and participate in raising saints?

Questions for Parents and Children

St. Monica's heart was weighed down by watching her son wander away from God's plan of holiness for his children. What does it feel like when someone you love makes a poor choice? How can you help them find a better way forward?

Venerable Ernesto Cofiño: Holiness in Work and Family Life

Venerable Ernesto Cofiño, born in 1899 in Guatemala City, studied medicine at the Sorbonne before pioneering pediatrics in Guatemala. In 1933, he married Clemencia, a teacher, and together they had five children and 21 grandchildren. Ernesto balanced his demanding career with a loving family life, calling his wife the relief, support, encouragement, and joy of their home.

Driven by compassion, Ernesto saw each patient – rich or poor – as made in Gods' image. He taught pediatric medicine and founded homes for expectant mothers, orphans, and street children. He led organizations to prevent child abuse, end child malnutrition and disease, fight tuberculosis, and end abortion in his country. Later joining Opus Dei, he deepened his faith through daily Mass and devotion to the rosary. Ernesto passed away on October 17, 1991, leaving a legacy of seeking holiness in the world through ordinary work and family life. He was declared venerable by Pope Francis on December 14, 2023.

Questions for Couples

Venerable Ernesto drew inspiration from his prayer life to make a real difference for others at home and in his work. How does the love of the Trinity between the Father, Son, and Holy Spirit overflow into our family? What does that mean or look like in practical terms?

Questions for Parents and Children

Although Venerable Ernesto gave all the credit for their beautiful home life to his wife, he was clearly involved as well. In what ways do we see dad's generosity and self-gift for our family? In what ways do we honor him for his role in our lives?

Images of Saints and Models of Married Love

Portraits by Tracy L. Christianson (www.portraitsofsaints.com), used with permission:

- **Saint Thomas More**
- **Saint Lorenzo Ruiz**
- **Venerable Pierre Toussaint**
- **The Holy Family**
- **Saints Louis and Zélie Martin**
- **Saint Agnes Lê Thị Thành**

Blesseds Luigi and Maria Beltrame Quattrocchi: Public domain family photo from 1905, the year they were married.

Our Lady, Untier of Knots: Johann Georg Melchior Schmidtner, circa 1700 (www.sankt-peter-am-perlach.de/knotenmadonna.htm).

Venerable Vittorio Trancanelli: Photo with his wife Rosalia ("Lia") Sabatini in 1997, courtesy of the *Tribunale Ecclesiastico Interdiocesano Umbro,* used with permission.

Patriarchs Tobiah and Sarah: Julius Schnorr von Carolsfeld, photograph from *Die Bibel in Bildern,* 1853 (www.alamy.com/stock-photo/2BNC73B.html), used with permission.

Servant of God Chiara Corbella Petrillo: Photo courtesy of www.ChiaraCorbellaPetrillo.org, used with permission of Enrico Petrillo.

Saint Monica: Portrait © John Nava 2025, used with permission.

Venerable Ernesto Cofiño: Photo with his wife Clemencia, taken in 1958 on their 25th wedding anniversary, © Prelature of the Holy Cross and Opus Dei, used with permission.

Prayers and Blessings for Married Life

3×5 Prayer for Married Couples

Each day, at morning or evening, take
five minutes to prayerfully do three things together:

1. Ask – How can I pray for you today?

2. Share – Here is what is on my heart today.
Please pray for me!

3. Appreciate – Acknowledge the ways your spouse
has loved you in the last 24 hours.

End with an "Our Father" together.

Amen.

Prayer for Greater Love in Families

Gracious God, help us to love each other fervently,
with all our hearts.

Grow our love so deep that it is able and willing to overcome
and forgive a multitude of misunderstandings and doubts.

Inspire a spirit of hospitality in each of us
and enable us to cheerfully share our home.

We acknowledge that you have given each of us spiritual gifts.
Help us to put our own interests aside
and use those gifts to serve one another well.
We will rely on the strength and energy you supply.

We pray that everything we do within this family
will bring you glory through the One who lives in us.

Amen.

Source: Adapted from a prayer by an unknown author.

Blessing for Children

Lord, our God,
out of the speech of little children
you have fashioned a hymn of praise.
Look with kindness on these children (this child)
whom the faith of the Church commends
to your tender care.

Your Son, born of the Virgin Mary,
gladly welcomed little children.
He took them in his arms, blessed them,
and held them up as an example for all.

We pray that you, Father,
will also send your blessing upon them (him/her),
so that they (he/she) may grow in Christian maturity
and, by the power of the Holy Spirit,
become Christ's witnesses (witness) in the world,
spreading and defending the faith.

We ask this through Christ our Lord.
Amen.

Morning Prayer for Elementary School Children

Heavenly Father, I offer you this day
all that I do and think and say,
uniting it with what was done
by Jesus Christ your only Son.

Jesus, shine through me
and be so in me
that every person I come in contact with
may feel your presence in my soul.

Amen.

Source: A traditional morning offering prayer, author unknown, combined with an excerpt from a prayer by John Henry Cardinal Newman.

Prayer of Married Couples

O Lord, our God,
we bless you and thank you
for taking our love into your hands.

Come into our lives and
help us to fulfill our mission of love.

Guide us to form our children
to become witnesses of your love
in our family and in the community.

Give us strength to overcome discouragement
and be ever with us to share our joys.

Lord, bless our love and our home.

Amen.

Source: Adapted translation of a prayer from ACI Prensa. Used with permission.

Prayer in Times of Economic Difficulties

Lord, you have created the entire universe
and have endowed the earth with sufficient riches
to feed all the people who inhabit it... Come to our aid.

Lord, you care for the lilies of the field and the birds of the sky,
you clothe them, nourish them, and make them prosper...
Show forth your providence over us.

Help us, O Lord: instill in our hearts
a sense of justice, honesty, and charity.
Take care of our family, as we confidently await
our daily bread from you.

Grant us patience and trust, so that we may more easily respond
to your divine grace, knowing in our hearts that your Fatherly love
watches over us, our worries, and our hopes.

Amen.

Source: Adapted translation of a popular prayer in Spanish, author unknown.

Prayer for Safe Travel for Families

Father God,
as we journey these next days,
keep us in your loving care.
Protect us from danger, from mechanical failure,
and from violent storms.

Make us wise and prudent around water and in the woods.
Give us respect for nature,
so that we neither defy its power nor defile its beauty.

Help us to be kind to one another
and to enter into the relaxation of this trip with joyful hearts.
May we return home more thankful, more generous,
and more mindful of your blessings.

We ask too, that you bless all travelers
with the same protection and kindness.
We pray this in the name of Jesus.

Amen.

Source: Author unknown.

Prayer for Those Hoping to Conceive or Adopt a Child

God our Creator,
by your love the world is filled with life,
through your generosity one generation
gives life to another,
and so are your wonders told and your praises sung.
We look to you in our love and in our need:
may it be your will that we bear (adopt) a child
to share our home and faith.
Loving God, be close to us
as we pray to love and do your will.
You are our God, nourishing us forever and ever.

Amen.

Source: USCCB, Catholic Household Blessings and Prayers, *p. 225. Used with permission.*

Blessing of Grandparents

Leader: Blessed be God, who is faithful through all generations.
R/. Blessed be God forever.

The leader introduces the blessing in these or similar words:

Grandparents are cherished members of our family. They bring gifts of wisdom, experience, and love and share with us their life of faith. We thank God for their example and ask that he bless them with happiness and good health.

After a time of silence, all join in prayers of intercession and in the Lord's Prayer. Then the leader prays:

Lord God almighty,
bless our grandparents with long life, happiness, and health.
May they remain constant in your love
and be living signs of your presence
to their children and grandchildren.
We ask this through Christ our Lord.
R/. Amen.

All make the sign of the cross as the leader concludes:

May God bless us and keep us
all the days of our lives.
R/. Amen.

Source: Adapted from USCCB, Catholic Household Blessings and Prayers, *pp. 191–192. Used with permission.*

Blessing of an Engaged Couple

In the name of the Father, and of the Son, and of the Holy Spirt.

R/. Amen.

Brothers and sisters,
let us praise our Lord Jesus Christ,
who loved us and gave himself up for us.

R/. Amen.

The one who presides says the prayer with hands joined; if, however, he is a Priest or Deacon, he says the prayer with hands extended:

We give you praise, O Lord,
who in your gentle wisdom call and prepare
your son and daughter N. and N.
to love each other.
Graciously strengthen their hearts, we pray,
so that, by keeping faith and pleasing you in all things,
they may come happily to the Sacrament of Marriage.
Through Christ our Lord.

R/. Amen.

May the God of love and peace
dwell within you,
direct your steps,
and strengthen your hearts in his love.

R/. Amen.

Source: Adapted from the English translation of The Order of Celebrating Matrimony © *2013, International Commission on English in the Liturgy Corporation, 222-235. Used with permission.*

Prayer for Vocations

Loving God,
you speak to us and nourish us
through the life of our church community.

In the name of Jesus, we ask you to
send your Spirit to us so that men and
women among us, young and old,
will respond to your call to service and
leadership in the Church and in the family.

We pray especially, in our day, for those who
hear your invitation to be a priest, a deacon,
a consecrated religious, or a spouse in marriage.

May those who are opening
their hearts and minds to your call
be encouraged and strengthened
through our enthusiasm in your service.

Amen.

Source: Adapted from a prayer by an unknown author.

Prayer for the Grace of Forgiveness in Marriage

Lord Jesus, in view of your infinite mercy,
we come before you today,
humbly asking for your grace
to forgive each other for any hurts and wrongs
we may have caused within our marriage.

Fill our hearts with your love and understanding,
allowing us to let go of resentment and bitterness,
and to embrace forgiveness as a path to healing.

Guide us to communicate openly and honestly,
to listen with compassion, and to prioritize the love
and commitment we undertook on our wedding day.

We surrender our marriage to your loving care,
asking that you strengthen our bond
and renew our commitment to one another.

Amen.

Prayer for Families

We bless your name, O Lord,
for sending your own incarnate Son
to become part of a family,
so that, as he lived its life,
he would experience its worries and its joys.

We ask you, Lord,
to protect and watch over this family,
so that in the strength of your grace
its members may enjoy prosperity,
possess the priceless gift of your peace,
and, as the Church alive in the home,
bear witness in this world to your glory.

We ask this through Christ our Lord.
Amen.

Prayer of Spouses for Each Other

Lord Jesus, grant that I and my spouse
may have a true and understanding love
for each other. Grant that we may both be
filled with faith and trust. Give us the grace
to live with each other in peace and harmony.

May we always bear with one
another's weaknesses and grow from
each other's strengths. Help us to forgive
one another's failings and grant us
patience, kindness, cheerfulness and the
spirit of placing the well-being of one
another ahead of self.

May the love that brought us together
grow and mature with each passing year.
Bring us both ever closer to you through our love
for each other. Let our love grow to perfection.

Amen.

Source: Reprinted with permission of Catholic Online, www.catholic.org.

Prayer for My Mother – A Child's Prayer

Dear Blessed Mother Mary,
help my mom to be a good mother.
Give her peace and wisdom, strength and courage,
grace and happiness. Be nearby when she needs help.
Keep her close to your Son, Jesus. Help me to always
show my mom how very much I love her.

Amen.

A Mother's Prayer for Her Children

Dear Lord, bless my children in their waking and sleeping,
in the food they eat, and in their play and study.

Grant them, O Lord, the right use of your graces and gifts
that in all they do, in every pursuit of their lives,
they may seek to give you glory
and come to share in your eternal joy.

Direct their steps, O Lord, and lead them along paths
that will bring them to you, in peace and love forever.

Amen.

Prayer for Mothers

Loving God,
as a mother gives life and nourishment to her children,
so you watch over your Church.
Bless our mother.
Let the example of her faith and love shine forth.
Grant that we, her family,
may honor her always
with a spirit of profound respect.
Grant this through Christ our Lord.
Amen.

Prayer for Fathers

God, you are the giver of all life,
human and divine.
Bless our father.
May he be the best of teachers for his children,
bearing witness to the faith
by what he says and does,
in Christ Jesus our Lord.
Amen.

Source: USCCB, Catholic Household Blessings and Prayers, *pp. 188-189. Used with permission.*

Cultivating a Love That Lasts with *Communio*

Cultivating a Love That Lasts:
Tips and Tools from Communio to Nurture Your Marriage

It's a special moment – that first look down the aisle on your wedding day. Looking into each other's eyes at the altar, exchanging vows, and committing to love one another for a lifetime. At first, your love seems shiny, new, and exciting, and it feels like you can conquer the world together. But over time, day-to-day life takes over, and those feelings might fade.

Think of your marriage as a beautiful garden – filled with sweet fruit trees, nourishing vegetables, stunning flowers, and delicious herbs. A garden is a lively, ever-changing ecosystem that thrives with daily care. This means watering, pruning vines, weeding, composting, and protecting it from invasive critters. Through it all, your dedication to the garden pays off as it blossoms and grows.

How much more so should you dedicate yourself to your marriage, the living sign of your love and faithfulness to your spouse? Like a garden, nurturing your marriage will bear lasting fruit for your relationship and family. Strong marriages build strong families – and with strong families, our Church has a bright future.

The Positive Impacts

Your mission today is to invest fully in loving your spouse. Hold nothing back. Children are a beautiful gift, yet your primary vocational call is matrimony. Research shows that marital satisfaction is associated with greater happiness, reduced depression, longer life expectancy, and greater professional and financial success.

In loving your spouse, you love your children and model the beauty of marriage for them. Stability in the home meets children's basic needs for safety and security. It also shapes their faith. Kids experience God's love first through their parents. A child who grows up in a loving home with married parents is more likely to be open to the Heavenly Father's love.

Practical Steps You Can Take

Studies show that couples who spend at least 8–12 hours a year on relationship enrichment are the least likely to divorce and the most likely to enjoy marital satisfaction. Two factors predict success: the ability to communicate effectively and to resolve conflicts. To practice each, we've included two short exercises—one on communication and one on conflict resolution. Each takes only 15–20 minutes.

Beyond this, date your spouse! You went on many outings while dating and engaged – why stop now? Having fun together through regular date nights is even more important when work and kids fill your schedule. Here are some tips to get you started:

- Put it on the calendar (or it likely won't happen).
- Hire a babysitter, ask a friend or family member to watch the kids, or prioritize getting the kids to bed early so you can have an in-house date.
- Go out to dinner, attend a local event, or have a movie or game night at home.

The activity matters less than the choice to invest in one another. Start today by taking one small step to invest in your relationship. Just like tending a garden, simple acts of love and commitment will nurture your marriage for a lifetime of happiness.

Communio *is partnering with all 12 California dioceses to help parishes evangelize through stronger marriages and families. Our parish-based model—credited with reducing divorce rates by 24% in Jacksonville, FL—equips parishes to become places where marriages thrive, families are supported, and faith takes root for generations. If you're interested in learning more about how Communio can work with your parish, visit* communio.org *or email Damon Owens at* dowens@communio.org.

Communication Exercise: Weekly Check-In

In the busyness of life, you and your spouse may slip into autopilot—living together yet out of sync. A weekly check-in can help you reconnect, get on the same page, and align your goals.

Directions: Take 10 minutes to have your first check-in. The goal of a weekly meeting is to clear the air of any issues so nothing gets bottled up, foster teamwork, ensure you both feel heard and cared for going into the week, and set your marriage and family agenda for the next seven days. **Make sure to put away phones, make eye contact, and be attentive to one another during this time.**

- Step 1: Show Gratitude — Start by choosing something you are grateful for this week and a way your spouse deserves to be appreciated.

  A highlight of my week was ______________________________.

  I appreciated when you ___________________________________.

  I feel most loved & supported when you ________________.

- Step 2: Identify Trouble Spots — Any tensions or issues that popped up this week? Take the time to discuss your feelings and listen to your spouse's. Ask your spouse:

  "Was there anything that bothered you this week that you'd like to discuss?"

  "Anything stressful coming up this week for you, and what do you need from me?"

  "Is there anything I can do to support you better?"

- Step 3: Sync Up the Family Calendar — Use a weekly planner to review and set next week's family priorities (including Weekly Goals, Upcoming Events, and Reminders)

- Step 4: Pray for Each Other — Ask your spouse:

  "Is there anything specific you want me to pray for?"

Then, take a moment to pray for each other right now. You can pray from the heart or use this Catholic prayer for spouses:

> *Lord Jesus, grant that my spouse and I may have a true and understanding love for each other. Grant that we may both be filled with faith and trust. Give us the grace to live with each other in peace and harmony. May we always bear with one another's weaknesses and grow from each other's strengths. Help us to forgive one another's failings, and grant us patience, kindness, cheerfulness, and the spirit of placing the well-being of one another ahead of self.*
>
> *May the love that brought us together grow and mature with each passing year and bring us both ever closer to you. Let our love grow to perfection. Amen.*

Lock in Your Weekly Check-Ins: Keep it going! Set a recurring day and time for your next weekly check-in. Make it fun! Grab a coffee or a special treat while you discuss.

Conflict Resolution Exercise: Giving and Receiving Apologies

Conflict in relationships is inevitable. Arguments happen, harsh words may be spoken, and apologies are needed. This exercise offers steps to give—and receive—a proper apology.

Directions: Take a moment on your own to reflect on a time when your partner hurt your feelings or did something to upset you. This could include something they did wrong or how they acted in an argument or discussion.

Start by sharing a moment or issue using "I" statements, e.g., "I feel _____ when you _____."

> *(Important: Make sure that the feelings are related to how you feel and that you are not making a "you" attack under the guise of "I feel." Avoid "I feel YOU..." statements.)*

Give Your Apology:

Now, the apologizing partner follows these four steps:

- Step 1: Acknowledge what your spouse says you did or said that bothered them.
- Step 2: Apologize for what you did or said or for how you came across. For example:

  "I am sorry for ________." Or "I am sorry for coming across as ________."
- Step 3: Briefly explain your motives and your perspective. Sometimes you can stop after Step 2, but if you feel compelled to explain, make it brief! Watch out for using "but" after you apologize—it can minimize the apology. Explain if you must, but make sure your focus is on the apology first and then on clarifying your motive.
- Step 4: If you explained your motive, apologize again. For example:

  "I am sorry for when I said ________. What I really meant was ________, but I am so sorry that I came across in an unappreciative way and hurt your feelings."

Accept the Apology:

Finally, the receiving partner should accept the apology. Some people feel so entitled to an apology that when they hear it, they might say, "Yeah, that WAAAS horrible of you."

Remember, it can be incredibly hard for the apologizing spouse to show humility and give a good apology. So, when you get one, RECEIVE it, BELIEVE it, and then ACCEPT it.

For clarity's sake, accept it by saying "I accept your apology" or "Thank you for your apology; I forgive you" or whatever it is you feel like saying, but acknowledge the apology.

This exercise is adapted from content created by Dr. Morgan Cutlip of LoveThinks. Learn more at www.lovethinks.com.

Radiate Love Through Social Media

Radiate Love Through Social Media

At the core of the *Radiate Love* initiative from the California Bishops is the conviction that marriage is the union of a man and a woman *in Christ*. As such, every sacramental marriage is called to be a reflection of God's covenant love for his people, patterned on the total, irrevocable, faithful, and life-giving sacrifice of Christ on the cross for the Church. Although our efforts to live out that Good News may not be perfect, they still shine forth is a guiding light for our world. So yes, we are called to *Radiate Love* through the witness of our own marriages, in word and deed.

Nowadays, messages on social media can easily be used to build up the people in our circles. The following are some ideas for sharing the *Radiate Love* message online. Add the words to your own photos or turn them into memes. Or even better, use your own creativity and your own words to expound on the beauty and goodness of sacramental marriage for couples and their family life. Whenever possible, add the hash tag **#RadiateLove** so that others can easily find your posts. Thank you for Radiating God's Love!

Simple Messages

Marriage radiates the love of God!

In the deepest core of our hearts, we want to love and be loved.

Marriage: It's romantic. It's authentic. It's an adventure!

Bear witness to the truth that God is love and love is from God.

Whatever you do, do everything for the glory of God (1 Corinthians 10:31).

Teach us the beauty of forgiveness and bearing one another's burdens.

I freely give my whole self to you, without holding anything back.

Love is forever because God is Love.

Deeper Thoughts

Join us in celebrating marriage as a beautiful journey of love. Let's embrace each day as an opportunity to strengthen our bonds, generously give our all, and radiate love in our homes and beyond.

Here's to the joy, strength, and blessings that come from walking hand in hand… for our own good, the good of our children, and the good of the world!

Every day, children bring the unexpected into our homes and families. In good times and bad, embrace their daily unpredictability as a gift from God!

The ups and downs of life are both better when we face them together. Embrace the adventure of a lifelong commitment!

When a marriage is able to stand the test of time, it is beautiful, transformative… a path of holiness that makes us more fully human.

The grace that Jesus still offers to couples in the Sacrament of Marriage is the gift of *abundant life* (John 10:10) through a covenant love that lasts a lifetime.

The mission of the family is to make disciples of our spouses and our children! Families, filled with the love of Jesus and love for each other, invite others to experience love and understand their own purpose.

Marriage is a vocation, a call put on one's heart by God, and a way to love that each person fulfills in a unique way. This vocation is truly a pilgrimage of faith and hope in love, because God has the map!

When the moment arrives to humbly give and receive forgiveness, the Holy Spirit pours out grace on our will so we can grow in holiness and love.

Jesus taught us to reconcile with those we have offended and always forgive those who have offended us. Asking for forgiveness regularly actually deepens our loving relationships.

Scripture Quotes

Jesus said to his disciples, "Whoever receives one child such as this in my name, receives me" (Mark 9:37). The Catholic community of Jesus' disciples is faithfully waiting: bring your child for Baptism!

"May the LORD bless you from Zion; / may you see Jerusalem's prosperity / all the days of your life, / and live to see your children's children" (Psalm 128). Love does last a lifetime – let your love shine!

"Come to me, all you who labor and are burdened, and I will give you rest" (Matthew 11:28).

Love "bears all things, believes all things, hopes all things, endures all things" (1 Corinthians 13:7).

"What God has joined together, no human being must separate" (Mark 10:9).

Papal and Magisterial Quotes

Love generously, especially when you feel you have nothing left to give. "God's way of loving becomes the measure of human love." – Pope Benedict XVI

"Authentic married love is caught up into divine love... so that this love may lead the spouses to God." – Second Vatican Council, Gaudium et Spes

"The family is, so to speak, the domestic Church. In it parents should, by their word and example, be the first preachers of the faith to their children." – Second Vatican Council, Lumen Gentium

"The family is the fundamental cell of society, where we learn to live with others despite our differences and to belong to one another; it is also the place where parents pass on the faith to their children." – Pope Francis

"Every family needs a father - a father who shares in his family's joy and pain, hands down wisdom to his children, and offers them firm guidance and love." – Pope Francis

"The good of the person, of society and of the Church herself passes by way of the family." – St. John Paul II

"Believe in love, believe in God, and believe that you are capable of taking on the adventure of a love that lasts a lifetime. Love wants to be permanent; 'until further notice' isn't love." – Pope Francis

Quotes from Saints

"If you want to bring happiness to the whole world, go home and love your family." – St. Teresa of Calcutta

"When a husband and wife are united in marriage, they no longer seem like something earthly, but rather like the image of God himself." – St. John Chrysostom

"Marriage is to help married people sanctify themselves and others. For this reason they receive a special grace in the sacrament which Jesus instituted. Those who are called to the married state will, with the grace of God, find within their state everything they need to be holy." - St. Josemaría Escrivá

"The loveliest masterpiece of the heart of God is the heart of a mother." – St. Thérèse of Lisieux

For World Marriage Day, the Second Sunday of February

Happy World Marriage Day! Let's embrace each day as an opportunity to strengthen our bonds, support one another, and spread love in our homes and beyond.

Today, we honor the beauty of marriage. Together, we thrive in love, faith, and unity. Let's cherish this journey where we grow, learn, and support each other. Here's to the joy, strength, and blessings that come from walking hand in hand. Happy World Marriage Day!

Celebrate World Marriage Day... Because together we thrive!